CHURCH
HISTORY
IN PLAIN LANGUAGE
Workbook

BRUCE L. SHELLEY

with STACEY SHELLEY LINGLE

Marshall Shelley, General Editor

ZONDERVAN
ACADEMIC

ZONDERVAN ACADEMIC

Church History in Plain Language Workbook
Copyright © 2022 by The Estate of Bruce L. Shelley

Published in Grand Rapids, Michigan, by Zondervan. Zondervan is a registered trademark of The Zondervan Corporation, L.L.C., a wholly owned subsidiary of HarperCollins Christian Publishing, Inc.

Requests for information should be addressed to customercare@harpercollins.com.

Zondervan titles may be purchased in bulk for educational, business, fundraising, or sales promotional use. For information, please email SpecialMarkets@Zondervan.com.

ISBN 978-0-310-13896-9 (softcover)
ISBN 978-0-310-13897-6 (ebook)

Cover design: Bruce Gore | Gore Studio, Inc.
Cover photos: Adobe Stock; ChristinePetro / Shutterstock; Unsplash; Public Domain
Interior design: Kait Lamphere

Printed in the United States of America

24 25 26 27 28 29 30 31 32 33 34 /TRM/ 15 14 13 12 11 10 9 8 7 6 5 4 3 2

CONTENTS

PART 1:

The Age of Jesus and the Apostles, 6 BC–AD 70

PART 2:

The Age of Catholic Christianity, 70–312

PART 3:

The Age of the Christian Roman Empire, 312–590

PART 4:

The Christian Middle Ages, 590–1517

PART 5:

The Age of the Reformation, 1517–1648

PART 6:

The Age of Reason and Revival, 1648–1789

PART 7:

The Age of Progress, 1789–1914

PART 8:

The Age of Ideologies, 1914–1989

PART 9:

The Age of Technology and the Spirit, 1990–

1

THE AGE OF JESUS AND THE APOSTLES

6 BC–AD 70

CHAPTER 1

AWAY WITH THE KING!

The Jesus Movement

1. What evidence supports the view of Jesus as a founder of the church?

2. What was the contemporary expectation of the prophesied Messiah?

3. On the map, label the following:

Nazareth   Jordan River   Samaria
Sea of Galilee   Galilee   Judea
Jerusalem

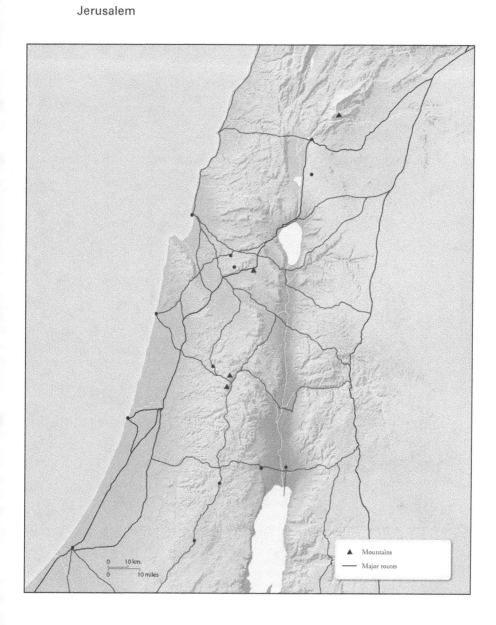

0   10 km.
0   10 miles

▲ Mountains
— Major routes

4. Match each Jewish faction with its characteristics.

Pharisees   Emphasized Jewish tradition and identity

Combined piety and patriotism

Sadducees

Represented wealthy, aristocratic families

Zealots   Likely responsible for the Dead Sea Scrolls

Members included chief priests and high priest

Essenes

Name means "separated ones"

Took armed resistance to Roman rule

Modeled themselves on the militant Maccabees

Little to no interest in politics

Enjoyed the sophisticated manners of Greco-Roman culture

Withdrew to Judean wilderness for monastic life

5. What was the main theme of Jesus' teaching?

6. Why did Jesus present real danger to both Sadducees and Pharisees?

7. How did Jesus frame his relationship to the covenant given to Israel at Mount Sinai?

CHAPTER 2

WINESKINS OLD AND NEW

The Gospel to the Gentiles

1. How does the story of Stephen reveal Christianity's perspective on its emergence from Judaism?

2. True or False: At Pentecost, Peter announced Jesus as Messiah by appealing to Jewish Scripture.

3. What were the two special ceremonies that the early church celebrated, and what were their meanings?

4. What encouraged the Jesus movement to spread beyond Jerusalem?

5. On the map, label the following sites.

- Early Christian communities

Jerusalem	Tarsus	Cyprus
Antioch	Damascus	Alexandria

- Paul's missionary journeys

Athens	Philippi	Ephesus
Corinth	Thessalon-	Rome
Galatia	ica	

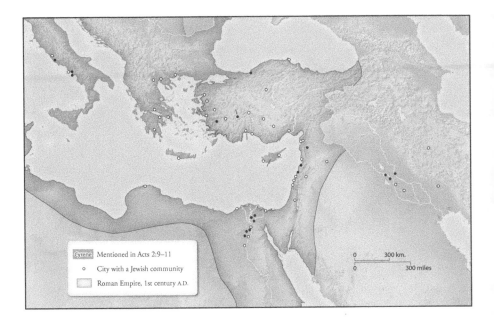

6. What issues created tension between Jewish and gentile Christians in first-century Christianity?

7. Why does the Jewish revolt of AD 66–70 mark a decisive rift between Judaism and Christianity?

PART 1 REVIEW

Discussion Questions

1. What might the reception to Jesus be if he appeared today instead of more than two thousand years ago? Would there be a modern-day equivalent of the Pharisees' and Sadducees' concerns?
2. How does modern-day Christianity view its relationship to Judaism? How has the relationship changed since Christianity's inception?

Writing Topics for Further Study

1. Many contemporary New Testament scholars contrast Jesus' emphasis on God's kingdom with Paul's emphasis on justification by faith. Examine the relevant Scriptures and describe the nature of the contrast. How do both emphases find expression in the Christian church?

Suggested Reading

Luke 4:14–21; Acts 9:1–20; 10:34–43; 1 Corinthians 1:10–17; 15:1–8

McKnight, Scot. "Jesus vs. Paul." *Christianity Today*, December 2010.

2. The Didache ("Teaching") is a Christian manual compiled by the earliest Christians, perhaps as early as the first century. Its statement of belief may be the first written catechism, and it reflects how Jewish Christians saw themselves and adapted their practices for gentile believers. Read the Didache and look for evidence of Christianity's Jewish roots. What presumptions of practice and belief does the author make? What new elements are prescribed for the nascent Christian church?

Suggested Reading

The Didache. New Advent: newadvent.org/fathers/0714.htm.

Kavanagh, Aidan. "Repeating the Unrepeatable." *Christian History* 37 (1993).

2

THE AGE OF CATHOLIC CHRISTIANITY

70–312

CHAPTER 3

ONLY "WORTHLESS" PEOPLE

Catholic Christianity

1. Define *catholic Christianity* as it is used in this chapter.

2. What circumstances served as "preparation for the gospel" in the gentile world?

3. After the fall of Jerusalem, what site functioned as the "home of Christianity"? Why?

4. True or False: Most of the thirty thousand Christians in Rome in AD 250 were from the upper classes.

5. In what way was the expansion of the early church in the Roman Empire "uneven"?

6. Briefly describe the work of the following early apologists.

- Irenaeus

- Tertullian

7. What four human factors contributed to the spread of the church in this period?

CHAPTER 4

IF THE TIBER FLOODS

The Persecution of Christians

1. What was Rome's general policy toward the religions of conquered peoples? Why was Christianity received differently?

2. How did Christians set themselves apart from Roman life?

3. True or False: Persecutions like that of Nero were common during the first and second centuries.

4. What were the two slanderous rumors about Christians that spread and raised suspicion?

5. Paraphrase the following quote from Tertullian's *Apology*.

> If the Tiber floods the city, or if the Nile refuses to rise, or if the sky withholds its rain, if there is an earthquake, a famine, a pestilence, at once the cry is raised: "Christians to the lion."

6. How did the tradition of emperor worship arise in Rome? Place the following steps in order.

_____ Caesar worship became imperial policy.
_____ The spirit of Rome was embodied by the emperor.
_____ Roman rule brought peace and justice to a territory.
_____ The growing empire needed a unifying force.
_____ Citizens were grateful to the spirit of Rome for their new security.

7. Why did the exaltation of the emperor create a problem for Christians?

CHAPTER 5

ARGUING ABOUT THE EVENT

The Rise of Orthodoxy

1. In addition to external threats, what served as a "subtler and no less critical" danger to Christianity in its early centuries?

2. Define the following terms.

    • Theology

    • Orthodoxy

3. What role does heresy play in the development of Christian orthodoxy?

4. What are some examples of early Christian theology drawing on Jewish language and concepts?

5. Early church members encountered the central truths of the faith in several ways, including hymns. Examine the following two creedal hymns and underline elements that fit the definition of *theology*.

- 1 Timothy 3:16

  > He appeared in the flesh,
  >> was vindicated by the Spirit,
  > was seen by angels,
  >> was preached among the nations,
  > was believed on in the world,
  > was taken up in glory.

- Philippians 2:5–11

  > In your relationships with one another, have the same mindset as Christ Jesus:

  > Who, being in very nature God,
  >> did not consider equality with God something to be used
  >>> to his own advantage;
  > rather, he made himself nothing
  >> by taking the very nature of a servant,
  >> being made in human likeness.
  > And being found in appearance as a man,
  >> he humbled himself
  >> by becoming obedient to death—
  >>> even death on a cross!

> Therefore God exalted him to the highest place
> > and gave him the name that is above every name,
> that at the name of Jesus every knee should bow,
> > in heaven and on earth and under the earth,
> and every tongue acknowledge that Jesus Christ is Lord,
> to the glory of God the Father.

6. What are the "two fronts" on which the gospel of John fights? Which two heresies are already shaping orthodoxy in the first and second centuries?

7. What did Gnosticism teach about the person and purpose of Jesus? Why was this teaching attractive to many people?

8. Which phrases in the Apostle's Creed repudiate the claims of Gnosticism?

CHAPTER 6

THE RULE OF BOOKS

Formation of the Bible

1. Define the following terms.

- Bible

- Testament (or covenant)

- Canon

2. Why did early believers immediately embrace the Old Testament (or Jewish Scriptures) as a Christian book?

3. In addition to the old covenant, what did Christians look to as their rule of faith?

4. Among the growing body of Christian literature, only twenty-seven books came to be set apart as Scripture. What three qualifications do they share?

5. What were the teachings of Marcion? How did the church respond to his challenges?

6. What were the teachings of Montanus? How did the church respond to his challenges?

7. When was the New Testament canon—the twenty-seven books as we have them today—first recorded?

    a. AD 185
    b. AD 256
    c. AD 313
    d. AD 367

CHAPTER 7

SCHOOL FOR SINNERS

A Structure That Fits

1. Define *episcopacy.*

2. Read 1 Timothy 3:1–10, Titus 1:5–9, and 1 Peter 5:1–3. Describe the church leadership structure Paul instructs. What roles and responsibilities were defined in the early church?

3. How did the challenge from Gnosticism move the church toward a single bishop (or pastor) in each local church?

4. What are the three Christian perspectives on this major shift in the structure of church authority?

5. The third century saw the church shift toward wider acceptance of repentant sinners, in contrast to previously strict standards for fellowship in the communion. What factors contributed to this shift?

6. Cyprian and Cornelius argued positions that centralized a system of forgiveness within the office of the bishop, and essentially established which third Catholic sacrament?

    a. Confirmation
    b. Eucharist
    c. Penance
    d. Holy orders

CHAPTER 8

APOSTLES TO INTELLECTUALS

Interacting with Other Worldviews

1. Define *Hellenism*.

2. What reasoning supports Tertullian's argument against Christian engagement with Greek philosophy?

3. Explain Clement's metaphor of truth as a river. What does it argue about Christianity and its relationship to Hellenism?

4. Some Christian converts perceived a choice "between clever, eloquently defended heresy and a seemingly ignorant orthodoxy." What was the "third possibility" Clement sought to provide?

5. How did Clement and Origen's approach differ from that of the heretical Gnostics?

6. Origen is known for his allegorical interpretations of Scripture. What convictions led him to this method?

Homilies on Luke

Study an example of Origen's allegorical method. Read the following parable from Luke and Origen's commentary on the passage. Identify the three levels of meaning he finds in the text.

LUKE 10:25–37

On one occasion an expert in the law stood up to test Jesus. "Teacher," he asked, "what must I do to inherit eternal life?"

"What is written in the Law?" he replied. "How do you read it?"

He answered, "'Love the Lord your God with all your heart and with all your soul and with all your strength and with all your mind'; and, 'Love your neighbor as yourself.'"

"You have answered correctly," Jesus replied. "Do this and you will live."

But he wanted to justify himself, so he asked Jesus, "And who is my neighbor?"

In reply Jesus said: "A man was going down from Jerusalem to Jericho, when he was attacked by robbers. They stripped him of his clothes, beat him and went away, leaving him half dead. A priest happened to be going down the same road, and when he saw the man, he passed by on the other side. So too, a Levite, when he came to the place and saw him, passed by on the other side. But a Samaritan, as he traveled, came where the man was; and when he saw him, he took pity on him. He went to him and bandaged his wounds, pouring on oil and wine. Then he put the man on his own donkey, brought him to an inn and took care of him. The next day he took out two denarii and gave them to the innkeeper. 'Look after him,' he said, 'and when I return, I will reimburse you for any extra expense you may have.'

"Which of these three do you think was a neighbor to the man who fell into the hands of robbers?"

The expert in the law replied, "The one who had mercy on him."

Jesus told him, "Go and do likewise."

FROM HOMILY 34, *HOMILIES ON LUKE*, ORIGEN

[. . .] But the teacher of the Law "wanted to justify himself" and show that no one was a neighbor to him. He said, "Who is my neighbor?" The Lord adduced a parable, which begins, "A certain man was going down from Jerusalem into Jericho," and so on. And he teaches that the man going down was the neighbor of no one except of him who willed to keep the commandments and prepare himself to be a neighbor to every one who needs help. For, this is what is found after the parable, at its end: "Which of these three does it seem to you is the neighbor of the man who fell among robbers?" Neither the priest nor the Levite was his neighbor, but—as the teacher of the Law himself answered—"He who showed pity" was his neighbor. Hence, the Savior says, "Go and do likewise."

[. . .] The man who was going down is Adam. Jerusalem is paradise, and Jericho is the world. The robbers are hostile powers. The priest is the Law, the Levite is the prophets, and the Samaritan is Christ. The wounds are disobedience, the beast is the Lord's body, the pandochium (that is, the stable), which accepts all who wish to enter, is the Church. And further, the two denarii mean the Father and the Son. The manager of the stable is the head of the Church, to whom its care has been entrusted. And the fact that the Samaritan promises he will return represents the Savior's second coming.

[. . .] The Samaritan, "who took pity on the man who had fallen among thieves," is truly a "guardian," and a closer neighbor than the Law and the prophets. He showed that he was the man's neighbor more by deed than by word. According to the passage that says, "Be imitators of me, as I too am of Christ," it is possible for us to imitate Christ and to pity those who "have fallen among thieves." We can go to them, bind their wounds, pour in oil and wine, put them on our own beasts, and bear their burdens. The Son of God encourages us to do things like this.

He is speaking not so much to the teacher of the Law as to us and to all men when he says, "Go and do likewise." If we do, we shall obtain eternal life in Christ Jesus, to whom is glory and power for ages of ages. Amen.

1. Literal meaning:

2. Moral application:

3. Allegorical or spiritual sense:

CHAPTER 9

COUNTRIES OF THE SUNRISE

Early Christianity in Asia and Africa

1. Instead of thinking of Christianity as migrating westward from its Palestinian beginnings, what is a more accurate description of the first millennium of Christianity's growth?

2. What doctrinal issue served to divide the church at the Council of Chalcedon in 451?

3. Match the Eastern church with the apostolic tradition linked to its founding.

Syria	Mark
Armenia	Thaddeus and Bartholomew
India	Phillip
Egypt	Thaddeus
Ethiopia	Thomas

4. On the map, label the following churches discussed in the text.

   a. Syria   c. Egypt   e. Ethiopia

   b. Armenia   d. Nubia

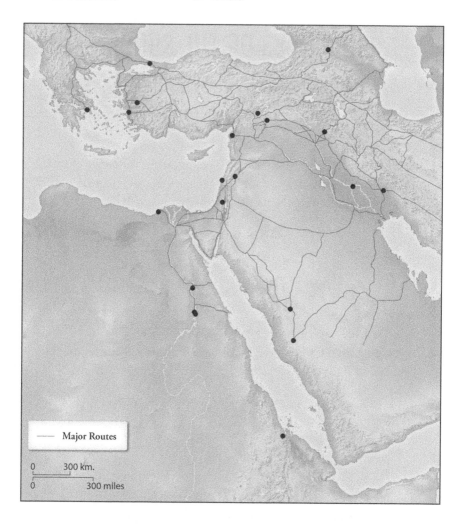

5. What "new power" contributed to the near destruction of many of these Eastern churches by the end of the fourteenth century?

30

PART 2 REVIEW

Discussion Questions

1. What are some theological debates ongoing today? Where do Christians look for authority on these debates?
2. The stories of the martyrs—Perpetua, Thecla, Polycarp, and others—often contain miraculous elements. How do you account for these extrabiblical miracle stories? Should they be considered mythical or historical? What affects your view?
3. How is church leadership organized today? How has it evolved further from the episcopacy of the second century? What are the strengths and weaknesses of modern models?

Writing Topics for Further Study

1. Read chapters 39–47 from Tertullian's *Apology*, his fiery defense of Christianity. He responds to Roman persecution and paints a prophetic portrait of Christian society. According to Tertullian, what are the characteristics of a Christian community within a hostile larger society? How can the church be "in the world," but not "of the world"? Consider any pastoral applications for today's church.
2. Choose an ecumenical council: Nicaea (325) or Chalcedon (451). What was the main doctrinal debate? What were the main positions taken? Examine the strengths and weaknesses of each position. What are the consequences of the position eventually established as orthodox?

3

THE AGE OF THE CHRISTIAN ROMAN EMPIRE

312–590

CHAPTER 10

LAYING HER SCEPTRE DOWN

Conversion of the Empire

1. What were the "signs of a crumbling empire" present in the years preceding Constantine's rule?

2. Describe the imperial attitude toward Christianity under Diocletian and Galerius.

3. What supernatural experience did Constantine claim to have during his battle at the Milvian Bridge?

4. Many suppose Constantine's conversion to be a purely political maneuver. What evidence supports Constantine's authentic Christian convictions?

5. Give at least three reasons Constantine chose to move the imperial capital to Constantinople, the former Byzantium.

6. The conversion of Constantine and the promotion of Christianity can be viewed as a "new age of salvation." What were some of the disadvantages to Christianity's new favored status?

7. As the emperor ascended to demigod status, what "weapon" did Western bishops maintain to keep them accountable to the church?

    a. Withholding taxes
    b. Excommunication
    c. Preaching against them
    d. Stoking civil unrest

CHAPTER 11

SPLITTING IMPORTANT HAIRS

The Doctrine of the Trinity

1. From Constantine's perspective, why was clarifying the doctrine of
the Trinity important?

2. Who was Arius and what did he believe about Jesus?

3. How was the Council of Nicaea (325) different from previous
meetings of church leaders?

4. Explain the importance of the term *homoousion* in the Nicene Creed.

5. For each of the two personal analogies for the Trinity, provide an example and the shortcomings.

- Social analogy

- Psychological analogy

6. Explain the use of the term *person* and what it would have meant to the early Christians.

Nicene Creed

Read the Nicene Creed (381) and highlight all phrases that respond to the theological challenges discussed in this chapter.

I believe in one God the Father Almighty; Maker of heaven and earth, and of all things visible and invisible.

And in one Lord Jesus Christ, the only-begotten Son of God, begotten of the Father before all worlds. God of God, Light of Light, very God of very God, begotten, not made, being of one substance with the Father; by whom all things were made; who, for us and for our salvation, came down from heaven, and was incarnate by the Holy Ghost of the Virgin Mary, and was made man; and was crucified also for us under Pontius Pilate; he suffered and was buried; and the third day he rose again, according to the Scriptures; and ascended into heaven, and sits on the right hand of the Father; and he shall come again, with glory, to judge both the quick and the dead; whose kingdom shall have no end.

And I believe in the Holy Ghost, the Lord and Giver of Life; who proceeds from the Father and the Son; who with the Father and the Son together is worshiped and glorified; who spoke by the Prophets. And I believe in one Holy Catholic and Apostolic Church. I acknowledge one Baptism for the remission of sins; and I look for the resurrection of the dead, and the life of the world to come. Amen.

CHAPTER 12

EMMANUEL!

Christ in the Creeds

1. Summarize the contrasting Christologies prevalent in Antioch and Alexandria in the early church.

2. How did the structure of the church evolve to include archbishops and patriarchs throughout the fourth and fifth centuries? How did the four patriarchs relate to each other?

3. Match each of the three heresies with its associated teacher.

Nestorius

Apollinaris

Eutyches

1. The divine Word displaced the animal soul, uniting with Jesus' body and creating a "unity of nature."

2. Mary is not the "God-bearer"; Jesus represents a merging of wills rather than an essential union.

3. Jesus' human and divine natures are combined so intimately that the human is lost in the divine.

4. Which of the following is *not* a key affirmation about Christ from the Council of Chalcedon (451)?

    a. Complete in Godhead and complete in manhood
    b. Two natures, without confusion, without change, without division
    c. Each nature being preserved and coming together to form one person
    d. Exactly half divine and half human

CHAPTER 13

EXILES FROM LIFE

Beginnings of Monasticism

1. How does the story of Anthony recounted in Athanasius's *Life of Saint Anthony* echo some of the Christian martyr stories told earlier?

2. How have Catholic and Protestant views on monasticism differed?

3. What examples of asceticism are found in the New Testament? Feel free to provide your own beyond the three cited.

4. What was the first form of monasticism and who was its prime example?

5. Why was there a correlation between the growing popularity of Christianity and the rise of monasticism?

6. What were the innovations of Pachomius's first Christian monastery?

7. Which figure embodies the emergence of monastic scholarship?

    a. Pachomius
    b. Anthony
    c. Jerome
    d. Basil

8. What benefits did Benedictine monasteries offer to Western Europe as Rome's power receded?

CHAPTER 14

THE SAGE OF THE AGES

Augustine of Hippo

1. Identify three influences on Augustine's conversion to Christianity.

2. Read the following statements. Decide whether each statement would be made by a Pelagian (P), a Donatist (D), or Augustine (A).

_____ a. A priest who allows Scripture to be burned is disqualified from service.

_____ b. The Catholic church is apostate and not the true church of Christ.

_____ c. A sacrament's validity rests in Christ, not in the minister.

_____ d. The church may need to use harsh action to suppress its rivals.

_____ e. Each person has total freedom to act sinfully or righteously.

_____ f. God does not predestine anyone for hell.

_____ g. Every person is "in Adam" and shares his fall from grace.

_____ h. All power to do good is the free gift of God (grace).

3. How did the sack of Rome affect Augustine's theological focus?

4. What are the key differences, according to Augustine, between the City of God and the Worldly City?

Confessions

Read the following excerpt from Augustine's *Confessions*, a story from his rebellious teenage years. Based on this anecdote, what does Augustine believe about sin?

> 2.4. Your law, Lord, surely punishes stealing, the law written in the hearts of man, which not even iniquity itself wipes out. For what thief calmly puts up with a thief? Not even a rich thief endures a thief who is driven by neediness. Yet I wanted to steal, and I did steal, driven by no need, but by the lack of and disdain for justice. For I stole that of which I had plenty and much better. Nor did I want to enjoy the thing which I desired to steal, but I enjoyed the stealing and sin themselves. There was a pear tree near our vineyard, loaded with fruit that was not enticing in shape or taste. We, most wicked youths, went to shake it down, and to carry off fruit in the middle of the night—we had prolonged our play that long out of evil custom. And we took large fruits, not to eat, but to at least throw to the pigs—even though we did eat some of it—we just wanted to do that which pleased us precisely because it was illicit. Behold my heart, O God, behold my heart, which you took pity on in the depth of the abyss. Let my heart now tell you what it was seeking there—so that it was evil without cause, and there was no cause for my malice but malice.

CHAPTER 15

PETER AS "PONTIFEX MAXIMUS"

Beginnings of the Papacy

1. Why is Leo a major figure in the development of the papacy?

2. Why was the church in Rome given prominence among the churches of the Western Empire? Give three reasons.

3. How did the Council of Constantinople (381) contribute to the church at Constantinople and the church at Rome heading in "different directions"?

4. How did Leo justify the primacy of the bishop of Rome?

5. What are three difficulties with Leo's claim?

6. What decision at the Council of Chalcedon (451) challenged Leo's vision of the papacy?

7. How did the looting of Rome by the Vandals (455) affect Leo's standing in the West?

CHAPTER 16

SOMEWHERE BETWEEN HEAVEN AND EARTH

Eastern Orthodoxy

1. What happened in 1054 and is known as the Great Schism?

2. What is the significance of icons to the Eastern Orthodox faith?

3. How does the concept of salvation differ between Eastern and Western Christianity?

4. How did Justinian see the relationship between Roman empire and Christian religion?

5. Explain the two sides in conflict in the iconoclastic controversy.

6. After the fall of Constantinople, in what geographic direction did Orthodoxy grow?

CHAPTER 17

BENDING THE NECKS OF VICTORS

Mission to the Barbarians

1. What event marks the end of Roman rule of the Western Empire, and why is this date somewhat artificial?

2. What characteristics and values broadly defined the culture of the German tribes?

3. How did the Arian Germans regard church structure, especially in contrast to the Roman tradition?

4. Describe the origins and influence of the Christian church in Ireland.

5. The story of Clovis is an example of the mass conversions that spread Christianity in northern Europe. How did these mass conversions shape the character of Christianity?

6. How did King Ethelbert of Great Britain respond to the missionary sent by Pope Gregory the Great?

7. True or False: Once Christianity was securely established in Anglo-Saxon England, the flow of missionaries reversed, and British missionaries were sent to Christianize the continent.

PART 3 REVIEW

Discussion Questions

1. British historian Hugh Trevor-Roper wondered, "Who can even guess what would happen to the world, or to Christianity, if the Roman Empire had not become Christian?" What do you think the consequences of Constantine's conversion were?

2. Constantine's religious experience and convictions had an enormous impact on how he governed his empire. Many historians argue his public faith was at least partially politically motivated. What is the relationship today between public religion and politics?

3. Anthony and the desert fathers and mothers pioneered Christian asceticism. Are there any streaks of asceticism remaining in modern Christianity? What practices of austerity and self-denial continue?

4. The word *icon* has expanded in meaning since the early centuries of Eastern Orthodoxy. Today, it can mean any person of influence. It can also refer to an image on a digital screen that links to an application or a file. How are these added meanings consistent with the original definition of *icon*? Do they reveal anything about changing attitudes toward the divine?

Writing Topics for Further Study

1. Research the beliefs of Jehovah's Witnesses (jw.org), a modern religion that promotes the teachings of Jesus. Compare their Christology with that of Arius, as described in chapter 11. Based on your findings, should Jehovah's Witnesses be considered Arians? Are there any significant distinctions in their view of Christ?

2. Pope Leo I builds his argument for the primacy of the bishop of Rome on a particular reading of Matthew 16. Read his "Sermon III" and analyze his interpretation. What assumptions is he making? Are there other interpretations available?

3. The Great Schism came about because of a complicated mix of theological and political tensions. One of the theological flash points was the wording of the Nicene Creed in a later revision. Research the

differing views on the *filioque* clause and analyze the importance of this three-word phrase in shaping Christian Trinitarian theology. Is there any evidence that its addition or omission has shaped Western and Eastern Christian practice over the centuries?

4

THE CHRISTIAN MIDDLE AGES

590–1517

CHAPTER 18

GOD'S CONSUL

Gregory the Great

1. What were the two sources of devastation in sixth-century Rome that cleared the way for the ascendancy of Christian Europe?

2. What personal qualifications did Gregory possess that prepared him for leadership at this crucial time of transition?

3. How did Gregory respond to the "presumption" of the patriarch of Constantinople calling himself "universal bishop"?

4. For the following theological statements, place a checkmark next to those that appear in Gregory's formulation of early Middle Ages Christianity:

    ____ a. Adam's fall affected all of his descendants.

    ____ b. Original sin destroys man's capacity for free will.

    ____ c. Once grace moves an individual, he or she may respond with good works.

    ____ d. Baptism grants grace to anyone, regardless of merit.

    ____ e. Even sins committed after baptism are forgiven because of the merit of baptism.

    ____ f. Penance is required to atone for any sins after baptism.

    ____ g. Jesus is the only intercessor between humans and God.

    ____ h. Holy relics may possess great powers, including that of self-defense.

    ____ i. Jesus' sacrifice allows all the baptized to enter heaven after death.

    ____ j. The bread and wine of the Eucharist are symbolic of Jesus' body and blood.

    ____ k. The Eucharist is effective penance for those who participate.

CHAPTER 19

THE SEARCH FOR UNITY

Charlemagne and Christendom

1. Define the term *Christendom.*

2. In the blending of Roman and Germanic cultures, how did the Franks rise to prominence?

3. Describe the relationship between Pepin and the pope. What benefit did each receive from the other?

4. List three lasting effects of the alliance between the papacy and the Franks.

5. True or False: The Christmas Day coronation of Charlemagne by Pope Leo III restored the Christian Roman Empire.

6. What was the relationship of church and state in Charlemagne's empire?

7. How did the rise of feudalism lead to the decay of the pope's office?

8. Define the two practices that Gregory VII prohibited:

- Simony

- Lay investiture

9. Which of Gregory VII's principles have modern relevance for Christians across denominational divides?

The Song of Roland

The Song of Roland is an eleventh-century epic poem, the oldest surviving work of French literature. It tells the story of Charlemagne ousting one of the last Muslim strongholds in Spain, the mountain city of Saragossa.

Read the first stanza of this poem, which introduces both Charlemagne and his foe, the Muslim King Marcilius. What medieval attitudes toward Islam can you detect?

> The king our Emperor Carlemaine,
> Hath been for seven full years in Spain.
> From highland to sea hath he won the land;
> City was none might his arm withstand;
> Keep and castle alike went down
> Save Saragossa, the mountain town.
> The King Marsilius holds the place,
> Who loveth not God, nor seeks His grace:
> He prays to Apollin, and serves Mahound;
> But he saved him not from the fate he found.[1]

---

1. Source: sourcebooks.fordham.edu/basis/roland-ohag.asp.

CHAPTER 20

LIFTED IN A MYSTIC MANNER

The Papacy and the Crusader

1. How did the architecture of medieval Gothic cathedrals echo the aims of the medieval church?

2. How did Pope Innocent III differ from his predecessors?

3. Provide one example from the text of the pope asserting authority over secular political leaders.

4. What were some inciting events that motivated the First Crusade (1095)?

5. True or False: During the Crusades, the church followed the principles of "just war" laid down by Augustine.

6. Why can the First Crusade be considered the most successful of the seven?

7. How did the Crusades influence the development of the church's practice of offering "indulgences"?

8. Which of the following long-range results of the Crusades proves them successful?

   a. Winning the Holy Land
   b. Checking the advance of Islam
   c. Healing the schism between Western and Eastern churches
   d. None of the above

9. According to the text, what was the most significant result of the Crusades?

CHAPTER 21

THE NECTAR OF LEARNING

Scholasticism

1. How did Gerbert of Rheims innovate the medieval educational model?

2. Paraphrase Peter Abelard's quotation: "The first key to wisdom is assiduous and frequent questioning . . . For by doubting we come to inquiry, and by inquiry we arrive at the truth."

3. Describe the earliest universities.

4. Provide three examples of matters governed by canon law.

5. How did Thomas Aquinas respond to rival thinkers (Aristotle, Averroes, Maimonides) gaining traction in his day?

6. For the following theological statements, place a checkmark next to those consistent with Aquinas's *Summa Theologica*.

_____ a. There are two fountains of knowledge of God: reason and revelation.

_____ b. Each person is a sinner in need of the grace of God for salvation.

_____ c. Saving grace arrives immediately upon confession of faith in Jesus Christ.

_____ d. The church observes two symbolic ordinances: baptism and communion.

_____ e. In the Lord's Supper, the bread and wine are changed into real body and blood.

_____ f. Most souls will experience purgatory before achieving heaven.

_____ g. The church may issue indulgences to relieve souls in purgatory.

CHAPTER 22

A SONG TO LADY POVERTY

Francis and the Apostolic Lifestyle

1. The movement of voluntary poverty in the twelfth and thirteenth centuries was a correction to . . .

2. Earlier poverty movements had found expression in monasticism. How was this medieval movement different?

3. How was heresy defined by the medieval church? Why would preachers of apostolic poverty be in danger of heresy?

4. Two of Francis's forerunners in the poverty movement—Arnold and Waldo—met with very different results. How did their efforts end up and why?

  • Arnold of Brescia

  • Peter Waldo

5. Why did the Cathari, or Albigenses, pose a unique threat to the Christian church?

6. What were the distinctives of the newly formed Dominican order?

7. How did the church justify the brutality of the Inquisition?

8. How was the Franciscan order different from prior movements emphasizing Christian poverty?

CHAPTER 23

CHAOS AND THE LAW OF NECESSITY

Decline of the Papacy

1. What changes in the European mindset challenged the idea of "Christendom" during the late Middle Ages?

2. What was the nature of the conflict between Boniface VIII and King Philip of France?

3. What was the lasting significance of the Anagni episode?

4. Place a checkmark next to the statements that describe how the Avignon captivity weakened the papacy:

    ____ a. It separated the papacy from the idea of apostolic succession.

    ____ b. The new papal palace was modest and unadorned.

    ____ c. It placed the papacy at the service of one nation, the French, above others.

    ____ d. Revenue from the Papal States dropped dramatically.

    ____ e. The pope was not able to distribute his writings as efficiently.

5. True or False: The Avignon popes continued to rely on the issue of indulgences to raise funds.

6. Define *conciliarism*.

7. The Great Papal Schism was resolved in 1417 by the Council of Constance. What was the great contradiction that the council introduced?

CHAPTER 24

JUDGMENT IN THE PROCESS OF TIME

Wyclif and Hus

1. How did John Wyclif's views on lordship (dominion) differ from the views of the church?

2. In response to the Great Papal Schism of 1378, what did Wyclif propose about the papacy?

3. Summarize Wyclif's controversial views on the following.

   • Membership in the church

- Accessibility of Scripture

- Transubstantiation

4. How did the teachings of English Wyclif come to influence the Bohemian preacher John Hus?

5. What happened to John Hus at the Council of Constance?

6. What do the stories of Proto-Protestants like Wyclif and Hus suggest about the reform of the papal church?

PART 4 REVIEW

Discussion Questions

1. Medieval cathedrals featured architecture that reflected a theological emphasis. Their severe angles and heights pointed upward to a God who was transcendent and powerful. Their naves suggested the hull of a ship that carried the faithful to safety. Think about the architecture of churches today. What theological emphases do they reflect?

2. The papacy of Innocent III was groundbreaking for its assumption of authority over secular leaders. Time and again, the popes of the thirteenth century intervened in political matters, choosing monarchs and deciding civil wars. Do religious leaders today hold any political influence? Should they?

Writing Topics for Further Study

1. Most historians consider the sermon preached by Pope Urban II at Clermont in 1095 to have been the spark that ignited the Crusades, a wave of military campaigns to wrest the Holy Land from Muslim control. Find a translation of the sermon online and read it carefully. What rhetorical strategies does Urban II employ? What motivations does he provide his listeners? Why was this sermon so effective at rousing an army?

2. St. Francis and his movement for evangelical poverty served as a counteroffensive to the growing wealth and influence of the church in the thirteenth century. Recent centuries have had their own divergent views on the place of wealth in the Christian life. Research "prosperity theology," a movement arising in the late twentieth century, and identify its prominent voices. What would St. Francis have to say to teachers of this prosperity gospel? Write an imagined conversation between Francis and one or more prosperity teachers.

Suggested Reading

Bowler, Kate. "Death, the Prosperity Gospel, and Me." *New York Times*, February 13, 2016.

Stafford, William S. "The Case for Downward Mobility." *Christian History* 42 (1994).

5

THE AGE OF THE REFORMATION

1517–1648

CHAPTER 25

A WILD BOAR IN THE VINEYARD

Martin Luther and Protestantism

1. List the four questions that Protestantism answers in a new way.

2. What revolutionary insight did Martin Luther have after studying Romans 1:17? What did it mean for the role of the Church of Rome?

3. What was the "spark that ignited the Reformation"?

4. How did Luther view the relationship between salvation and good works, especially in contrast to the church's traditional teaching?

5. How did Luther spend his time as a fugitive hiding in Wartburg Castle?

6. List three ways Christian worship changed under Luther's reforms.

7. What are Luther's "invigorating new answers" to the four questions listed in question 1?

Augsberg Confession

The Augsberg Confession was drafted in 1530 as a presentation of Lutheran beliefs to Emperor Charles V. It includes twenty-one chief articles of faith, as well as seven statements describing what the authors viewed as abuses of the Christian faith present in the Roman Catholic Church.

Read the following selection from the Confession, and underline the assertions that depart from medieval Catholic teaching.

Article IV: Justification. We teach that men cannot be justified before God by their own strength, merits or works, but are freely justified for Christ's sake through faith, when they believe that they are received into favor and that their sins are forgiven for Christ's sake, who by His death has made satisfaction for our sins. This faith God accounts as righteousness in His sight, Rom. 3 and 4.

Article V: The Ministry of the Church. That we may obtain this faith, the ministry of teaching the Gospel and administering the sacraments was instituted. For through the Word and sacraments, as through instruments, the Holy Spirit is given, who works faith where and when it pleases God in those who hear the Gospel. That is, God, not because of our own merits, but for Christ's sake, justifies those who believe that they are received into favor for Christ's sake.

Article VI: New Obedience. We teach that this faith is bound to bring forth good fruits, and that it is necessary to do good works commanded by God because it is God's will. Yet we should not rely on those works to merit justification before God. For the forgiveness of sins and justification are apprehended by faith, as the words of Christ attest, "When you have done all those things which you are commanded, say, 'We are unprofitable servants'" [Luke 17:10]. The same is also taught by the Fathers. For Ambrose says, "It is ordained of God that he who believes in Christ is saved, freely receiving remission of sins, without works, by faith alone."

Article VII: The Church. We teach that one holy Church is to continue forever. The Church is the congregation of saints, in which the Gospel is rightly taught and the sacraments rightly administered. And concerning the true unity of the Church, it is enough to agree concerning the doctrine of the Gospel and the administration of the sacraments. Nor is it necessary that human traditions, rites, or ceremonies, instituted by men, should be the same everywhere. As St. Paul says, "One faith, one baptism, one God and Father of all," etc. [Eph. 4:5–6].

CHAPTER 26

RADICAL DISCIPLESHIP

The Anabaptists

1. What does the name "Anabaptists" mean? How did the group receive it? Why might it not be accurate, in their view?

2. How did the Anabaptists' desired reforms compare to the reforms of Lutheranism?

3. What did Ulrich Zwingli and the Anabaptists have in common? On which points did they disagree? What was the result of their disagreement?

4. Who was the first Anabaptist martyr? How many followed during the Reformation years?

5. What theological emphasis did Menno Simons contribute to the Anabaptist movement?

6. List the four major Anabaptist convictions outlined in the Schleitheim Confession.

CHAPTER 27

THRUST INTO THE GAME

John Calvin and Reformed Rule

1. How did John Calvin come to be the leader of the Reformation in Geneva?

2. Compare the central doctrines of Luther and Calvin.

3. What is the significance of Calvin's work *Institutes of the Christian Religion*?

4. What was life in Geneva like under John Calvin's leadership? Check all that apply.

    ___ a. All citizens had to make a confession of faith.

    ___ b. All citizens had to participate in a theological education program.

    ___ c. All were subject to excommunication for failure to conform to spiritual standards.

    ___ d. Drinking, gambling, and dancing were forbidden.

    ___ e. Reading of the Scriptures was forbidden.

    ___ f. At least one heretic was burned at the stake.

    ___ g. Priests were forbidden to marry.

5. What three tests constituted Calvin's "yardstick" for judging those likely to be among God's elect?

6. For Calvin, what is the relationship between justification and good works? (Is this distinct in any way from Luther's view in chapter 25)?

7. How did Calvinism, preached by John Knox, lead to civil war in Scotland?

CHAPTER 28

THE CURSE UPON THE CROWN

The Church of England

1. How did King Henry VIII's marital problems lead to England renouncing papal authority and establishing the Church of England?

2. What were the two serious changes that marked the new way of the Church of England under Henry VIII?

3. Though he was burned at the stake before seeing his work finished, what did William Tyndale contribute to the English Reformation?

4. Summarize the religious attitudes and influence of the three monarchs to follow Henry VIII.

- Edward VI

- Mary

- Elizabeth

5. Describe the terms of the *Via Media*, Elizabeth's middle way between Protestantism and Catholicism.

CHAPTER 29

"ANOTHER MAN" AT MANRESA

The Catholic Reformation

1. Who was Ignatius of Loyola and what led to his rebirth at Manresa?

2. After the sack of Rome in 1527, Pope Paul III turned to serious efforts at reform. Name two actions he took to respond to calls for change.

3. What did Ignatius teach about the path to spiritual perfection?

4. What was the Society of Jesus and what was its mission?

5. For each of the following Protestant values, provide the Council of Trent's responding view.

- Justification is by faith alone.

- Righteousness is external, from God.

- Salvation is by grace alone.

- Religious authority is in Scripture alone.

- No papal authority

- Two sacraments (ordinances)

- Preaching of the Word is central to worship.

6. As a result of these intractable differences, the Reformation reached its "second stage." What understanding grew as a result of the Council of Trent?

7. The future belongs, it is argued, to the "third stage" of religious plurality. What shift in the role of religion is required?

CHAPTER 30

OPENING THE ROCK

Uttermost America and Asia

1. Define the following two approaches to missionary activity in the Americas and the Far East.

   • The policy of adaptation

   • The policy of conquest

2. How did the legacy of the Crusades affect the European Christian attitude toward evangelism?

3. What were the characteristics and outworkings of Spain's policy of *encomienda*? Was it effective at spreading Christianity?

4. How did Francis Xavier's approach to missions in Japan differ from his earlier work in India?

5. What were the considerable barriers to missionary work in China? How did Matthew Ricci overcome them?

6. What caused the decline of the mission in China after Ricci and Schall's advances?

CHAPTER 31

THE RULE OF THE SAINTS

Puritanism

1. What is the modern connotation of the word *puritan* and why is that meaning a poor representation of the original Puritanism?

2. Summarize the three stages of Puritanism in England.

- Under Queen Elizabeth (1558–1603)

- Under James I and Charles I (1603–42)

- Under civil war and Oliver Cromwell (1642–60)

3. How did the Puritans arrive at the sense that God had a special place for the English people in his plan? What was this plan?

4. What were the characteristics of Puritan Separatism? What did a group of about a hundred Separatists do in September 1620?

5. How did Puritans in England respond to Charles I and Archbishop William Laud's enforcement of high-church Anglicanism?

6. The Puritans, led by Oliver Cromwell, did overthrow and abolish the English monarchy in 1649, but their time in power (the "protectorate") was brief. What does the text suggest was the error in their tactics?

Westminster Confession of Faith

The Westminster Confession of Faith was drafted at the Westminster Assembly by Puritan leaders in an effort to reform the Church of England even further from its Catholic influences. This statement became, and still serves as, a standard of doctrine for Presbyterian and Congregationalist churches.

The following excerpt from chapter 7, "Of God's Covenant with Man," provides an example of the Puritans' distinctive "covenant theology." As you read, look for definitions of "covenant of works" and "covenant of grace." What is meant by these terms? What were the historical consequences of the Puritans' view of themselves as "God's new Israel"?

1. The distance between God and the creature is so great, that although reasonable creatures do owe obedience unto him as their Creator, yet they could never have any fruition of him as their blessedness and reward, but by some voluntary condescension on God's part, which he hath been pleased to express by way of covenant.

2. The first covenant made with man was a covenant of works, wherein life was promised to Adam; and in him to his posterity, upon condition of perfect and personal obedience.

3. Man, by his fall, having made himself incapable of life by that covenant, the Lord was pleased to make a second, commonly called the covenant of grace; wherein he freely offereth unto sinners life and salvation by Jesus Christ; requiring of them faith in him, that they may be saved, and promising to give unto all those that are ordained unto eternal life his Holy Spirit, to make them willing, and able to believe.

4. This covenant of grace is frequently set forth in Scripture by the name of a testament, in reference to the death of Jesus Christ the Testator, and to the everlasting inheritance, with all things belonging to it, therein bequeathed.

5. This covenant was differently administered in the time of the law, and in the time of the gospel: under the law, it was administered by promises, prophecies, sacrifices, circumcision, the paschal lamb, and other types and ordinances delivered to the people of the Jews, all foresignifying Christ to come; which were, for that time, sufficient and efficacious, through the operation of the Spirit, to instruct and build up the elect in faith in the promised Messiah, by whom they had full remission of sins, and eternal salvation; and is called the old testament.

6. Under the gospel, when Christ, the substance, was exhibited, the ordinances in which this covenant is dispensed are the preaching of the Word, and the administration of the sacraments of baptism and the Lord's Supper: which, though fewer in number, and administered with more simplicity, and less outward glory, yet, in them, it is held forth in more fullness, evidence and spiritual efficacy, to all nations, both Jews and Gentiles; and is called the new testament. There are not therefore two covenants of grace, differing in substance, but one and the same, under various dispensations.[1]

---

1. Full text available at opc.org/wcf.html.

CHAPTER 32

UNWILLING TO DIE FOR AN OLD IDEA

Denominations

1. In the mid-sixteenth century, a stalemate between Protestants and Catholics led to the adoption of the territorial principle. What was the territorial principle?

2. True or False: Territorialism heralded an end to wars of religion and brought an unprecedented era of peace in Europe.

3. The Thirty Years' War ended with the Peace of Westphalia. What was the religious consequence of that treaty?

4. In the American colonies, what religious policy did England adopt which attracted colonists to settle new lands? Name a few examples of groups that benefited from this policy.

5. The Puritans were the exception to the rule, with an insistence on religious conformity. Even so, what were several factors that undercut Puritan intolerance?

6. According to the text, what is the difference between sectarianism and denominationalism?

7. Outline the denominational theory articulated by the Dissenting Brethren of Westminster.

"A Model of Christian Charity"

John Winthrop, the first governor of the Massachusetts Bay Colony, delivered a sermon to his fellow Puritan settlers before they landed in New England in 1630. This sermon, titled "A Model of Christian Charity," is famous for its use of the phrase "city on a hill," a reference to Jesus' Sermon on the Mount and a vision of the planned Puritan community.

As you read the following excerpt from the sermon, look for Winthrop's description of the required Christian conformity, a Puritan distinctive. How does he justify the rigid rule of the Puritan saints?

> Thus stands the cause between God and us. We are entered into covenant with Him for this work. We have taken out a commission. The Lord hath given us leave to draw our own articles. We have professed to enterprise these and those accounts, upon these and those ends. We have hereupon besought Him of favor and blessing. Now if the Lord shall please to hear us, and bring us in peace to the place we desire, then hath He ratified this covenant and sealed our commission, and will expect a strict performance of the articles contained in it; but if we shall neglect the observation of these articles which are the ends we have propounded, and, dissembling with our God, shall fall to embrace this present world and prosecute our carnal intentions, seeking great things for ourselves and our posterity, the Lord will surely break out in wrath against us, and be revenged of such a people, and make us know the price of the breach of such a covenant.
>
> Now the only way to avoid this shipwreck, and to provide for our posterity, is to follow the counsel of Micah, to do justly, to love mercy,

to walk humbly with our God. For this end, we must be knit together, in this work, as one man. We must entertain each other in brotherly affection. We must be willing to abridge ourselves of our superfluities, for the supply of others' necessities. We must uphold a familiar commerce together in all meekness, gentleness, patience and liberality. We must delight in each other; make others' conditions our own; rejoice together, mourn together, labor and suffer together, always having before our eyes our commission and community in the work, as members of the same body. So shall we keep the unity of the spirit in the bond of peace. The Lord will be our God, and delight to dwell among us, as His own people, and will command a blessing upon us in all our ways, so that we shall see much more of His wisdom, power, goodness and truth, than formerly we have been acquainted with. We shall find that the God of Israel is among us, when ten of us shall be able to resist a thousand of our enemies; when He shall make us a praise and glory that men shall say of succeeding plantations, "may the Lord make it like that of New England." For we must consider that we shall be as a city upon a hill. The eyes of all people are upon us. So that if we shall deal falsely with our God in this work we have undertaken, and so cause Him to withdraw His present help from us, we shall be made a story and a by-word through the world. We shall open the mouths of enemies to speak evil of the ways of God, and all professors for God's sake. We shall shame the faces of many of God's worthy servants, and cause their prayers to be turned into curses upon us till we be consumed out of the good land whither we are going.

And to shut this discourse with that exhortation of Moses, that faithful servant of the Lord, in his last farewell to Israel, Deut. 30. "Beloved, there is now set before us life and death, good and evil," in that we are commanded this day to love the Lord our God, and to love one another, to walk in his ways and to keep his Commandments and his ordinance and his laws, and the articles of our Covenant with Him, that we may live and be multiplied, and that the Lord our God may bless us in the land whither we go to possess it. But if our hearts shall turn away, so that we will not obey, but shall be seduced, and worship other Gods, our pleasure and profits, and serve them; it is propounded unto us this day, we shall surely perish out of the good land whither we pass over this vast sea to possess it.

Therefore let us choose life, that we and our seed may live, by obeying His voice and cleaving to Him, for He is our life and our prosperity.

PART 5 REVIEW

Discussion Questions

1. The final sentence of chapter 26 argues that the four principles of Anabaptism, once punishable by death, have gone mainstream. They are now widely embraced by Christians of all expressions. Review those four principles and evaluate that argument. Which of these principles are central to mainstream Christianity today? Which are not?
2. Consider the spiritual exercises of Ignatius of Loyola. Which sound helpful to you? Which do not? Have you ever practiced anything like this and what was your experience?
3. Chapter 32 describes the rise of denominationalism. Think about the various Christian denominations present in your community. How do they interact? Have you seen any evidence that the denominations view themselves as members of a larger group—the church?

Writing Topics for Further Study

1. Watch the 2003 film *Luther*, paying special attention to the character of Prince Frederick. In the film, what seem to be his motivations in protecting Luther? How does the film depict the interplay of religious and political interests? After reading about the political climate surrounding Luther's agitation, evaluate the historicity of the film's Frederick.

   Suggested Reading
   Spitz, Lewis. "The Political Luther." *Christian History* 34 (1992).

2. After Francis Xavier's successful mission to Japan, the Tokugawa shogunate expelled all missionaries and banned Christianity in 1614. Thousands of believers were martyred and some went underground to survive. Japanese Christianity didn't make a public appearance again until a Christian (Kirishitan) community was discovered near Nagasaki in the 1860s.

   Read *Silence* by Shusaku Endo or view the 2016 Martin Scorsese film of the same name for a fictional depiction of Japanese Christianity under seventeenth-century persecution. Reflect on what Christianity looks like stripped of its European cultural context and legal protections. What parts of the Catholic faith are central, and must be preserved, to the Japanese Kirishitans? What is influenced by culture?

3. Sociologists have argued that Puritan ethics and ideas influenced the development of capitalism. Consider the Puritan theology and its journey across the Atlantic. Is there a connection between Reformed theology and the pursuit of vocational success? Or is this theory an erroneous myth? Read various perspectives and make an argument of your own about the relationship between Puritan theology and its economic consequences.

Suggested Reading

Barnes, Kenneth J. "Self-Serving Vice or Society-Building Virtue?" *Christian History* 137 (2020).

Ryken, Leland. "The Original Puritan Work Ethic." *Christian History* 89 (2006).

———. "That Which God Hath Lent Thee." *Christian History* 19 (1988).

Weber, Max. *The Protestant Work Ethic and the Spirit of Capitalism.*

6

THE AGE OF REASON
AND REVIVAL

1648–1789

CHAPTER 33

AIMING AT THE FOUNDATIONS

The Cult of Reason

1. Charles Williams describes the Age of Reason as a time when "national interests and mental relaxations combined to exclude metaphysics from culture." Paraphrase this definition.

2. What was the relationship of reason and religious authority during the Middle Ages? How did that change during the Age of Reason?

3. Define the term *Renaissance.*

4. For each of the following statements, write a response from an Enlightenment perspective.

- Humans are hopelessly sinful.

- The church is divinely instituted and the only hope for the world.

- The workings of nature are mysterious and evidence of God's activity.

5. How did John Locke harmonize faith and reason?

6. How did Voltaire's critique of the church differ from previous heretics or dissenters?

7. What response to deism did Bishop Joseph Butler offer? How effective was it?

CHAPTER 34

THE HEART AND ITS REASONS

Pascal and the Pietists

1. What was Jansenism's critique of Catholicism? What was its proposed correction?

2. What pivotal experience led Blaise Pascal to join the Jansenist movement and begin his theological writings?

3. What were the twofold aims of the Pietists?

4. Define the term *conversion* as understood by the Pietists. What did August Francke's conversion experience look like?

5. List four contributions Pietism made to Christianity worldwide.

6. What is the relationship between Pietism and the later evangelical Christian movement?

Pensées

Read this short excerpt, Pensée 100, from Blaise Pascal's *Pensées*. Underline the Jansenist position. What does Pascal believe about the nature of man? What is meant by the term *heart*?

Truly it is an evil to be full of faults; but it is a still greater evil to be full of them, and to be unwilling to recognise them, since that is to add the further fault of a voluntary illusion. We do not like others to deceive us; we do not think it fair that they should be held in higher esteem by us than they deserve; it is not then fair that we should deceive them, and should wish them to esteem us more highly than we deserve.

Thus, when they discover only the imperfections and vices which we really have, it is plain they do us no wrong, since it is not they who cause them; they rather do us good, since they help us to free ourselves from an evil, namely, the ignorance of these imperfections. We ought not to be angry at their knowing our faults and despising us; it is but right that they should know us for what we are, and should despise us, if we are contemptible.

Such are the feelings that would arise in a heart full of equity and justice. What must we say then of our own heart, when we see in it a wholly different disposition? For is it not true that we hate truth and those who tell it us, and that we like them to be deceived in our favour, and prefer to be esteemed by them as being other than what we are in fact? One proof of this makes me shudder. The Catholic religion does not bind us to confess our sins indiscriminately to everybody; it allows them to remain hidden from all other men save one, to whom she bids us reveal the innermost recesses of our heart, and show ourselves as we are. There is only this one man in the world whom she orders us to undeceive, and she binds him to an inviolable secrecy, which makes this knowledge to him as if it were not. Can we imagine anything more charitable and pleasant? And yet the corruption of man is such that he finds even this law harsh; and it is one of the main reasons which has caused a great part of Europe to rebel against the Church.

How unjust and unreasonable is the heart of man, which feels it disagreeable to be obliged to do in regard to one man what in some measure it were right to do to all men! For is it right that we should deceive men?

CHAPTER 35

A BRAND FROM THE BURNING

Wesley and Methodism

1. The Evangelical Awakening of the 1730s featured many leaders and spanned many regions, but all shared what common concern?

2. How did John Wesley come to be labeled a "Methodist"?

3. Describe Wesley's experience at the Aldersgate meeting.

4. What influence did the following groups and figures have on John Wesley's developing ideas?

  - Moravians

  - Jonathan Edwards

  - George Whitefield

5. How did John Wesley differ theologically from all other prominent leaders of the Great Awakening?

6. How did Wesley and his British followers relate to the Church of England?

7. How did Methodism's spread in America affect the trajectory of the whole movement?

CHAPTER 36

A NEW ORDER OF THE AGES

The Great Awakening

1. For thirty generations, Christianity existed in a working harmony with state authority. Why was this model impossible in nearly all of the new American colonies?

2. After the Puritan "holy experiment" failed to sustain a Christian covenantal society in New England, how was the new Massachusetts Charter of 1691 different from its predecessor?

3. Describe George Whitefield's methods and significance to the Great Awakening.

4. What does the phrase "new light" mean in the context of the Great Awakening? What did it mean to the traditional parish-church model?

5. What was the Baptist position on the relationship between church and state?

6. How did the revivalists of the Great Awakening find common ground with the Enlightenment thinkers moving toward the American Revolution? What ideology did they share?

"Sinners in the Hands of an Angry God"

"Sinners in the Hands of an Angry God" by Jonathan Edwards is the most famous example of the revival sermons delivered by itinerant preachers during the Great Awakening. This powerful preaching yielded dramatic responses, with listeners sobbing and gasping in the congregation.

As you read the following excerpt, look for the techniques and themes that might have elicited such a strong response. Underline metaphors and imagery that bring Edwards' theology to life. Why were sermons like these so effective in igniting religious fervor?

Your wickedness makes you as it were heavy as lead, and to tend downwards with great weight and pressure towards hell; and if God should let you go, you would immediately sink and swiftly descend and plunge into the bottomless gulf, and your healthy constitution, and your own care and prudence, and best contrivance, and all your righteousness, would have no more influence to uphold you and keep you out of hell, than a spider's web would have to stop a falling rock. . . .

The wrath of God is like great waters that are dammed for the present; they increase more and more, and rise higher and higher, till an outlet is given; and the longer the stream is stopped, the more rapid and mighty is its course, when once it is let loose. It is true, that judgment against your evil works has not been executed hitherto; the floods of God's vengeance have been withheld; but your guilt in the mean time is constantly increasing, and you are every day treasuring up more wrath; the waters are constantly rising, and waxing more and more mighty; and there is nothing but the mere pleasure of God, that holds the waters back, that are unwilling to be stopped, and press hard to go forward. If God should only withdraw his hand from the flood-gate, it would immediately fly open, and the fiery floods of the fierceness and wrath of God, would rush forth with inconceivable fury, and would come upon you with omnipotent power; and if your strength were ten thousand times greater than it is, yea, ten thousand times greater than the strength of the stoutest, sturdiest devil in hell, it would be nothing to withstand or endure it.

The bow of God's wrath is bent, and the arrow made ready on the string, and justice bends the arrow at your heart, and strains the bow, and it is nothing but the mere pleasure of God, and that of an angry God, without any promise or obligation at all, that keeps the arrow one moment from being made drunk with your blood. Thus all you that never passed under a great change of heart, by the mighty power of the Spirit of God upon your souls; all you that were never born again, and made new creatures, and raised from being dead in sin, to a state of new, and before altogether unexperienced light and life, are in the hands of an angry God. . . .

The God that holds you over the pit of hell, much as one holds a spider, or some loathsome insect over the fire, abhors you, and is dreadfully provoked: his wrath towards you burns like fire; he looks upon you as worthy of nothing else, but to be cast into the fire; he is of purer eyes than to bear to have you in his sight; you are ten thousand times more abominable in his eyes, than the most hateful venomous serpent is in ours. You have offended him infinitely more than ever a stubborn rebel did his prince; and yet it is nothing but his hand that holds you from falling into the fire every moment. It is to be ascribed to nothing else, that you did not go to hell the last night; that you were suffered to awake again in this world, after you closed your eyes to sleep. And there is no other reason to be given, why you have not dropped into hell since you arose in the morning, but that God's hand has held you up. . . .

And now you have an extraordinary Opportunity, a Day wherein Christ has flung the Door of Mercy wide open, and stands in the Door calling and crying with a loud Voice to poor Sinners; a Day wherein many are flocking to him, and pressing into the Kingdom of God; many are daily coming from the East, West, North and South; many that were very lately in the same miserable Condition that you are in, are in now an happy State, with their Hearts filled with Love to Him that has loved them and washed them for their Sins in his own Blood, and rejoicing in Hope of the Glory of God.

PART 6 REVIEW

Discussion Questions

1. The Great Awakening, and especially the preaching of revivalists like Whitefield and Edwards, promoted the place of emotion in the religious conversion experience. We've read the record of coal miners weeping at Bristol, and Edwards' audiences sobbing and gasping. In your experience, what is the role of emotion in spiritual life?

2. John Wesley, suffering from insecurity and disappointment in his faith, received the advice to "preach faith till you have it and then because you have it, you will preach faith." Is this good advice? What does the story of John Wesley suggest about the level of certainty required for Christian ministry?

Writing Topics for Further Study

1. Voltaire, a notorious Enlightenment-era critic of the church, once summed up his objection to religion: "Those who can make you believe absurdities can make you commit atrocities." How could the church respond to such a characterization? Prepare a logical response. What is Voltaire misunderstanding, misrepresenting, or omitting in his provocative maxim?

2. Consider the lyrics to two of Charles Wesley's hymns: "And Can It Be" and "Arise My Soul Arise." What common themes can you identify? What emphases are particularly reflective of the Evangelical Awakening?

7

THE AGE OF PROGRESS

1789–1914

CHAPTER 37

RESTORING THE FORTRESS

Catholicism in the Age of Progress

1. What did the Bastille represent? In its destruction, what new era was inaugurated?

2. What threat in the new era did Alexis de Tocqueville perceive? How did the Church of Rome respond to this threat?

3. Define the three demands of the French Revolution as described in the text.

   • Liberty

   • Equality

- Fraternity

4. What were the consequences of the French Revolution for the Church of Rome in France?

5. What were the consequences of liberalism for the Papal States in Italy?

6. What was significant and controversial about Pope Pius IX's 1854 declaration of Mary's immaculate conception?

7. What was the overall effect of the First Vatican Council (1870)?

CHAPTER 38

A NEW SOCIAL FRONTIER

Nineteenth-Century England

1. Jesus' prayer for the church in John 17 is that they would be "in the world" but not "of the world." How does the text explain the application of these phrases?

2. The increasing liberties of the age allowed for the formation of religious societies. How did they differ from churches?

3. What was the mission of the Clapham community?

4. What was the Claphams' twofold strategy for their campaign against slavery? How effective was it?

5. What was the mission of the Oxford movement?

6. How did the Oxford Anglicans' view of the church differ from the Clapham emphasis?

CHAPTER 39

TO EARTH'S REMOTEST PEOPLE

Protestant Missions

1. What new approach to Protestant missions did William Carey pioneer?

2. How did Andrew Fuller fit foreign missions within a Calvinist framework of election?

3. Why were the initial decades of the new missionary era predominantly evangelical?

4. How did eschatology, in addition to obedience to the Great Commission, motivate the Protestant missionary effort?

5. How did voluntary missionary societies differ from the church's previous missionary activity?

CHAPTER 40

THE DESTINY OF A NATION

A Christian America?

1. What were the two instruments evangelical Christians used to influence the American West?

2. What were the characteristics of the "camp meeting"?

3. The deadliest poison to the dream of a Christian America was the practice of slavery. Even Christians could not agree on what the Bible said on the subject. How did some (erroneously) attempt to justify slavery from biblical texts?

4. How did Harriet Beecher Stowe draw on Christian eschatology in her antislavery novel, *Uncle Tom's Cabin*?

5. What was the significance of the emergence of black churches during and after slavery? Which biblical texts provided special meaning to the black experience?

6. List three cultural shocks for Christians in the nineteenth century.

7. What were the two main evangelical responses to these cultural headwinds?

CHAPTER 41

A BRIDGE FOR INTELLIGENT MODERNS

Protestant Liberalism

1. What was the central aim of liberal theology?

2. Define the following theological terms. Which enjoyed greater emphasis from the Protestant liberals?

- Immanence

- Transcendence

3. Why were Darwin's ideas so challenging to many religious people? What doctrines, in particular, were threatened?

4. Place a checkmark next to each of the following that were concerns of biblical criticism.

       ___ a. Author's identity
       ___ b. Cultural context
       ___ c. Proving the Bible wrong
       ___ d. Geographic setting
       ___ e. Revisions and redactions
       ___ f. Modernizing the text

5. What is the "search for the historical Jesus"? What findings do these "searches" generally yield?

6. In lieu of a waning reliance on the Bible and historical orthodoxy, what did theologians like Friedrich Schleiermacher propose as the basis of the Christian faith?

7. According to theologian Albrecht Ritschl, modern religion needed to be practical, not theoretical. In this view, how does Jesus save? And what is salvation?

CHAPTER 42

NOTHING TO LOSE BUT CHAINS

Slums and the Social Gospel

1. Summarize the *laissez faire* economic philosophy that dominated during the Industrial Revolution. What effects did it have on urban laborers?

2. What was Karl Marx's response to the inequality proliferating under industrialization?

3. What was the Catholic response to the social crisis, as outlined in *Rerum Novarum*? What were its critiques of both Marxism and unfettered capitalism?

4. Why was the Church of England unable to respond effectively to the changing needs of society?

5. How did Christian Socialists adapt Marx's ideas to fit a Christian framework? What did they claim about the nature of the universe?

6. True or False: The social gospel, in advocating social reform, continued in the tradition of earlier American revivalism.

7. According to Walter Rauschenbusch, why is an individualistic gospel inadequate?

PART 7 REVIEW

Discussion Questions

1. Chapter 38 introduces the terms *low church* and *high church* to describe contrasting Christian attitudes toward sacrament and ritual. This continuum continues to describe the range of worship styles in the Protestant tradition today. Which approach are you more familiar with? What can each learn from the other?

2. William Carey's passion was to inspire his fellow Englishmen to take the gospel abroad. His writings carefully dismantle every popular objection to this important work. He believed foreign missions to be no less urgent than foreign trade, and we all know how successful and resilient global commerce has been since Carey's day. What are some modern objections to missionary work? How might they be addressed today?

Writing Topics for Further Study

1. The abolitionist work of William Wilberforce is dramatized in the 2006 film *Amazing Grace*. Watch the film and write a review that evaluates the presentation of Wilberforce's evangelical beliefs. According to the film, what is the relationship between Wilberforce's faith and activism? Does this seem to be accurate according to the facts of history?

2. The 1891 papal encyclical *Rerum Novarum* responds to the warring ideologies of the nineteenth and twentieth centuries. Read the document and identify the church's position on both free-market capitalism and socialism. What were Pope Leo's main critiques of each? In comparison, examine Pope Francis's 2020 encyclical *Fratelli Tutti*. How does Francis echo and extend the church's warnings regarding market capitalism?

8

THE AGE OF IDEOLOGIES

1914–1989

CHAPTER 43

GRAFFITI ON A WALL OF SHAME

Twentieth-Century Ideologies

1. What three post-Christian ideologies arose in the twentieth century? What did all have in common?

2. Describe the response to Nazism from the following Christian groups.

    • Catholics

    • German Christians

- Confessing Church

3. In what ways did Communism mirror Nazism? What were the key differences?

4. Describe the response to Soviet Communism from the following Christian groups.

- Russian Orthodox Church

- Catholics

5. How did Stalin's position toward the church shift during World War II?

6. What was the overall impact of World War II on Christianity?

7. How did each side in the Cold War receive support from its Christian population?

CHAPTER 44

ROOTLESS IMMIGRANTS IN A SICK SOCIETY

American Evangelicals

1. Define the following Protestant labels.

- Mainline

- Fundamentalist

- Pentecostal

- Evangelical

2. Explain Dwight L. Moody's lifeboat ethic, which represented a new evangelical approach to social engagement.

3. What is premillennialism and how did it help evangelicals interpret the events of the twentieth century?

4. List some new denominations that arose from modernist-fundamentalist differences.

5. Read the following example of the modernist view of Scripture. Underline the hallmarks of liberal theology present in it.

> The modernist uses Scripture as the trustworthy record and product of a developing religion. . . . In discovering this experience of God and accepting it as his own religious ancestry, the modernist affirms the trustworthiness of the Scripture . . . Christianity becomes not the acceptance of a literature but a reproduction of attitudes and faith, a fellowship with those ancient men of imperfect morals whose hearts found God.
>
> —Shailer Mathews, *The Faith of Modernism* (1924)

6. Read the following example of the fundamentalist view of Scripture. Underline the hallmarks of early fundamentalism present in it.

> The Bible not only gives us history, and that, too, written in many cases long after the events transpired, but it gives us prophecy which was fulfilled centuries later. The language of the Bible cannot be explained by environment, for environment, in most instances, was entirely antagonistic. It cannot be explained by genius of the writers, for they were largely among the unlettered. . . . The attacks upon it probably outnumber the attacks made upon all other books combined, because it condemns man to his face, charges him with being a sinner in need of a Saviour, indicts him as no other book does, holds up before him the highest standard ever conceived, and threatens him as he is threatened nowhere else.
> —William Jennings Bryan, *Seven Questions in Dispute* (1924)

7. What does the passage and repeal of the Eighteenth Amendment (Prohibition) reveal about cultural attitudes toward traditional morality?

8. How did a "new style of evangelicalism" position itself in relation to liberalism and fundamentalism after World War II?

CHAPTER 45

NEW CREEDS FOR BREAKFAST

The Ecumenical Movement

1. What is conciliar ecumenism?

2. What does the text label "the most ambitious expression of ecumenism"?

3. Another expression of the ecumenical movement was in the formation of denominational mergers and international alliances. Describe one such example.

4. What were the criticisms of conciliar ecumenism from conservative evangelicals?

5. What was the significance of the 1974 Lausanne conference?

Lausanne Covenant

Read the following excerpt from the 1974 Lausanne Covenant. Underline any distinctively evangelical emphases you find. Where do various evangelical traditions seem to find unity?

We, members of the Church of Jesus Christ, from more than 150 nations, participants in the International Congress on World Evangelization at Lausanne, praise God for his great salvation and rejoice in the fellowship he has given us with himself and with each other. We are deeply stirred by what God is doing in our day, moved to penitence by our failures and challenged by the unfinished task of evangelization. We believe the gospel is God's good news for the whole world, and we are determined by his grace to obey Christ's commission to proclaim it to all mankind and to make disciples of every nation. We desire, therefore, to affirm our faith and our resolve, and to make public our covenant.

1. The Purpose of God. We affirm our belief in the one eternal God, Creator and Lord of the world, Father, Son and Holy Spirit, who governs all things according to the purpose of his will. He has been calling out from the world a people for himself, and sending his people back into the world to be his servants and his witnesses, for the extension of his kingdom, the building up of Christ's body, and the glory of his name. We confess with shame that we have often denied our calling and failed in our mission, by becoming conformed to the world or by withdrawing from it. Yet we rejoice that, even when borne by earthen vessels, the gospel is still a precious treasure. To the task of making that treasure known in the power of the Holy Spirit we desire to dedicate ourselves anew.[1]

---

1. Full text available at lausanne.org.

CHAPTER 46

THE MEDICINE OF MERCY

Roman Catholicism and Vatican II

1. What image of the church was suggested by the Council of Trent? What image was introduced at Vatican II? Why is this shift a "revolution"?

2. What did Pope John XXIII mean by *aggiornamento*, the announced purpose of the Second Vatican Council?

3. For the following issues under consideration at Vatican II, outline the conservative and progressive positions.

   • Language of the liturgy

- Sources of divine revelation

- Church authority structure

4. As progressive views on church authority spread, what were the two cultural issues that threw the Catholic church into "extreme tension"?

5. Why might Vatican II have unintentionally sparked a major exodus of Catholic clergy?

PART 8 REVIEW

Discussion Questions

1. The Scopes trial, dramatized in the play *Inherit the Wind*, sets up a conflict between faith and science as sources of authority. The lesson, both from the play and from the historical aftermath, seems to be that scientific thinking triumphs in the modern public sphere. In your experience, how can this perceived tension be navigated? Where do you see the confrontation of science and religion today?

2. The term *evangelical* has come to have a kaleidoscopic meaning in American discourse—it seems to shift depending on the perspective. What are the varying meanings or connotations that you've encountered? Should the term be replaced to avoid all the confusion? What would it take to reclaim it?

Writing Topics for Further Study

1. Dietrich Bonhoeffer was a German Lutheran pastor and key founder of the Confessing Church. His resistance to the Nazi regime ultimately cost him his freedom, and then his life. Read some excerpts from his writings and a brief biography. How did he apply his theological convictions to his life?

Suggested Reading
Bonhoeffer, Dietrich. *The Cost of Discipleship.*
———. "Daring Thoughts." *Christian History* 32 (1991).
Kelly, Geffrey B. "Life and Death of a Modern Martyr." *Christian History* 32 (1991).

2. George Orwell's 1945 novella *Animal Farm* is a pointed allegory of Russia's Bolshevik Revolution, set on a farm populated by talking livestock. Read Orwell's fable and locate the character representing the Russian Orthodox Church in the allegory. What role does it play in the unfolding dystopia? What might Orwell be arguing about the Orthodox Church's place in the events of the twentieth century?

3. It has been more than fifty years since Vatican II, and the Catholic Church faces new challenges in a secular world. Today, the church hierarchy is still reeling from clerical sex-abuse scandals across the world. There's a shortage of priests, and church attendance is low. Polls show that large numbers of Catholics—even majorities in some countries—no longer follow church teaching on sexual morality. Is it time for Vatican III? Make an argument for a new ecumenical council and propose the top priorities the Catholic Church must address to reach the current age.

Suggested Reading

Perriello, Pat. "The Church Needs Vatican III." *National Catholic Reporter,* January 25, 2019. www.ncronline.org/news/people/ncr-today/church-needs -vatican-iii.

9

THE AGE OF TECHNOLOGY AND THE SPIRIT

1990–

CHAPTER 47

NEW TECHNOLOGIES, NEW CONTEXTS

Christian Ministries in the West

1. How has the Christian church embraced the digital transformation? What related challenges has it faced?

2. What strategies did the megachurch, or seeker-sensitive, movement employ to achieve church growth? What are some critiques of the megachurch model?

3. Provide several examples of the secularization of society in the late twentieth and early twenty-first centuries.

4. In addition to external pressures, the church also faced destabilizing internal developments. Provide one example.

5. What impact did the global refugee crisis of the early twenty-first century have on Western Christianity?

6. Explain the argument that the Pentecostal movement moved not only vertically but also horizontally.

CHAPTER 48

MORE PEOPLES, MORE TONGUES

Emergence of the Global South

1. On the map, indicate the areas described as the "Global South."

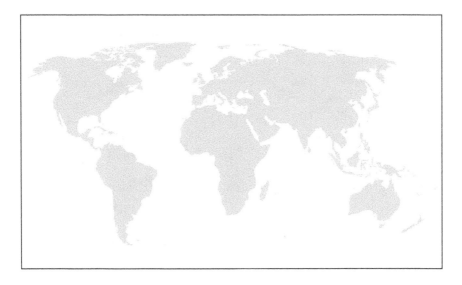

2. Which two forces suppressed early indigenous Christianity in the Global South?

3. How did the teachings of Vatican II lead to an indigenous Latin
American response to growing social unrest?

4. What were the forces constricting Christianity's growth in China
during the twentieth century? How did the church survive?

5. True or False: The world's largest church, by attendance, is in South
Korea.

6. How can we explain the rapid spread of Pentecostal Christianity in
the Global South?

7. What was the status and trajectory of Christianity in the Middle East in the twentieth and early twenty-first centuries?

8. What are the benefits and challenges of urbanization for Christianity?

PART 9 REVIEW

Discussion Questions

1. Where do you see evidence of the digital transformation on Christian practice? Or perhaps better, where *don't* you? What elements of church life have resisted transformation?

2. From G. K. Chesterton's *Heretics*: "The man who lives in a small community lives in a much larger world. . . . The reason is obvious. In a large community we can choose our companions. In a small community our companions are chosen for us." Do you see any truth in this quote? How does this apply to church experience? What has been your own experience of companionship in the church setting, either large or small?

Writing Topics for Further Study

1. The megachurch movement arising in the late twentieth century made use of new technologies and modern consumer attitudes, but was the form itself really an innovation? Or did it merely update a model evangelicalism had been using for decades? Consider various perspectives on the question and make an argument: What about megachurches was truly new, and what was a recontextualization of a received tradition?

Suggested Reading

Eagle, David E. "Historicizing the Megachurch." *Journal of Social History*, April 2015.

Schaller, Lyle. "Megachurch!" *Christianity Today*, March 5, 1990.

2. Research the life of Oscar Romero, a Salvadoran priest canonized in 2018, and write a "Profile of Faith" in the style of those included in the text. What role does his life play in the ongoing story of the Christian church?

ANSWER KEY

Most questions require a free response, based on the text. The following are answers to the multiple-choice, matching, and labeling questions.

CHAPTER 1

2. The locations on the map should be labeled as on the next page.
4. Characteristics for each faction are:
    - Pharisees
        Emphasized Jewish tradition and identity
        Combined piety and patriotism
        Name means "separated ones"
    - Sadducees
        Represented wealthy, aristocratic families
        Enjoyed the sophisticated manners of Greco-Roman culture
        Members included chief priests and high priest
    - Zealots
        Took armed resistance to Roman rule
        Modeled themselves on the militant Maccabees
    - Essenes
        Little to no interest in politics
        Withdrew to Judean wilderness for monastic life
        Likely responsible for the Dead Sea Scrolls

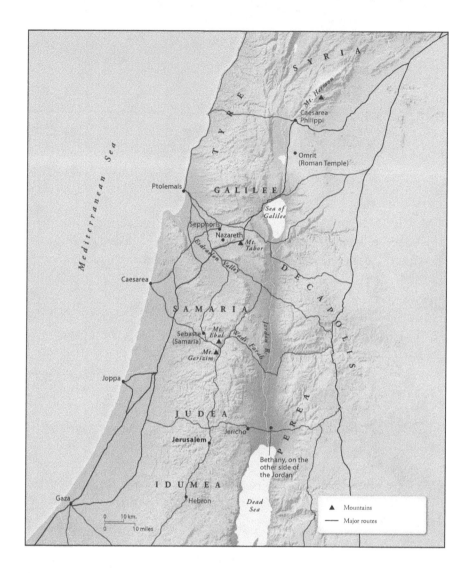

CHAPTER 2

2. True
5. The locations on the map should be labeled as follows:

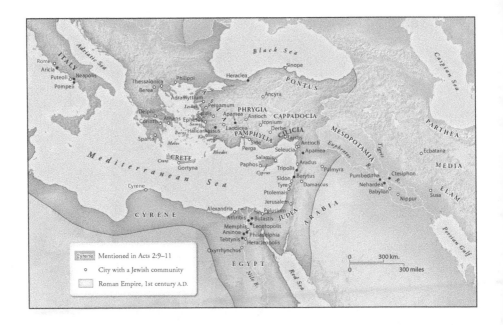

CHAPTER 3

4. False

CHAPTER 4

3. False
6. The correct order is:
    1. Roman rule brought peace and justice to a territory.
    2. Citizens were grateful to the spirit of Rome for their new security.
    3. The spirit of Rome was embodied by the emperor.
    4. The growing empire needed a unifying force.
    5. Caesar worship became imperial policy.

CHAPTER 6

7. D

CHAPTER 7

6. C

CHAPTER 9

3. The correct matches are:
   - Syria—Thaddeus
   - Armenia—Thaddeus and Bartholomew
   - India—Thomas
   - Egypt—Mark
   - Ethiopia—Phillip

4. The locations on the map should be labeled as follows:

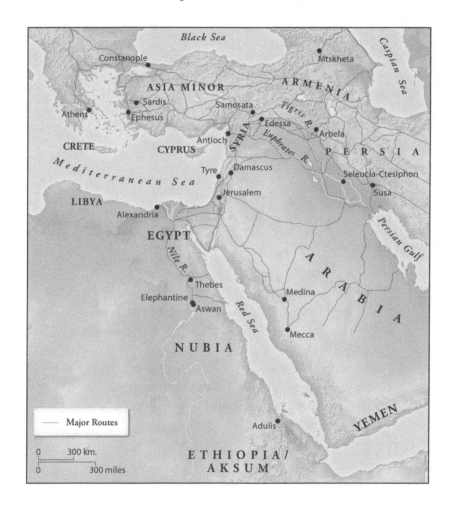

CHAPTER 10

7. B

CHAPTER 12

3. The correct matches are:
   Nestorius—B
   Apollinaris—A
   Eutyches—C
4. D

CHAPTER 13

7. C

CHAPTER 14

2. The correct matches are:

a. D	d. A	g. A
b. D	e. P	h. A
c. A	f. P	

CHAPTER 17

7. True

CHAPTER 18

4. Checkmarks should appear next to the following statements:
   a. Adam's fall affected all of his descendants.
   c. Once grace moves an individual, he or she may respond with good works.
   d. Baptism grants grace to anyone, regardless of merit.
   f. Penance is required to atone for any sins after baptism.
   h. Holy relics may possess great powers, including that of self-defense.
   k. The Eucharist is effective penance for those who participate.

CHAPTER 19

5. True

CHAPTER 20

5. False
8. D

CHAPTER 21

6. Checkmarks should appear next to the following statements:
   a. There are two fountains of knowledge of God: reason and revelation.
   b. Each person is a sinner in need of the grace of God for salvation.
   e. In the Lord's Supper, the bread and wine are changed into real body and blood.
   f. Most souls will experience purgatory before achieving heaven.
   g. The church may issue indulgences to relieve souls in purgatory.

CHAPTER 23

4. Checkmarks should appear next to the following statements:
   a. It separated the papacy from the idea of apostolic succession.
   c. It placed the papacy at the service of one nation, the French, above others.
   d. Revenue from the Papal States dropped dramatically.
5. True

CHAPTER 27

4. Checkmarks should appear next to the following statements:
   a. All citizens had to make a confession of faith.
   b. All citizens had to participate in a theological education program.
   c. All were subject to excommunication for failure to conform to spiritual standards.
   d. Drinking, gambling, and dancing were forbidden.
   f. At least one heretic was burned at the stake.

CHAPTER 32

2. False

CHAPTER 41

4. Checkmarks should appear next to the following statements:
   a. Author's identity
   b. Cultural context
   d. Geographic setting
   e. Revisions and redactions

CHAPTER 42

6. True

CHAPTER 48

1. Areas in the Global South are Latin America, Africa, Asia, and Oceania:

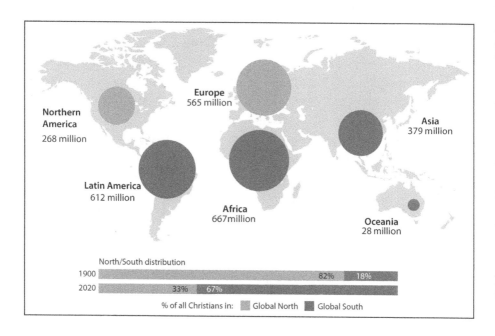

5. True

Church History in Plain Language 5th Edition

Bruce L. Shelley (author),
Marshall Shelley (revision editor)

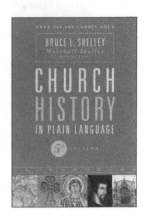

The story of the church for today's readers.
(Over 330,000 copies sold!)

Bruce Shelley's classic history of the church brings the story of global Christianity into the twenty-first century. Like a skilled screenwriter, Shelley begins each chapter with three elements: characters, setting, and plot. Taking readers from the early centuries of the church up through the modern era, he tells a story of actual people in a particular situation, provides a window into the circumstances and historical context, and develops the story of a major period or theme of Christian history.

For this fifth edition, Marshall Shelley brought together a team of historians, historical theologians, and editors to revise and update his father's classic text. The new edition adds important stories of the development of Christianity in Asia, India, and Africa, both in the early church as well as in the twentieth and twenty-first centuries. It also highlights the stories of women and non-Europeans who significantly influenced the development of Christianity but whose contributions are often overlooked in overviews of church history.

This concise book provides an easy-to-read guide to church history with intellectual substance. The new edition of *Church History in Plain Language* promises to set a new standard for readable church history.

Available in stores and online!